ABRAHAM
Father of Nations

Written and Illustrated

by

Pauline Shone

Olive Shoots
Imprint of
OlivePress
צהר זית
Publisher

Abraham, Father of Nations

"Feed My Sheep" Series

Written and Illustrated by Pauline Shone

Copyright © 2008, 2025 by Pauline Shone, Simon Books

Derbyshire, England

ISBN: 978-0-9554445-5-5

All rights reserved. No part of this book may be reproduced or transmitted in any form or by any means—electronic, mechanical, photocopying, or any information stored in a retrievable system,—without the prior permission of the copyright holder, according to USA and UK copyright laws.

Published by
Olive Shoots
an Imprint of:
Olive Press Publisher
www.olivepresspublisher.com
olivepressbooks@gmail.com

All Scripture quotes are taken from the *Holy Bible, New Living Translation*, copyright © 1996, 2004, 2015 by Tyndale House Foundation. Used by permission of Tyndale House Publishers, Inc., Carol Stream, Illinois 60188. All rights reserved.

All pronouns referring to the Trinity are capitalized.

Table of Contents

Foreword	9
God Calls Abram	10
Abram's Adventures Begins	12
Abram Arrives in Canaan	14
Abram Goes Down to Egypt	18
God Frightens Pharaoh	24
Abram Returns to Canaan	26
Abram and Lot Separate	28
Abram Stays in Canaan	30
Lot Is Taken Captive	34
Abram Rescues Lot	34
Abram Is Blessed by The King of Jerusalem	36
God Will Reward Abram	40

Hagar and Ishmael	42
Sarai Will Have Her Own Son	44
Abraham's Three Visitors	48
Sodom and Gomorrah	52
Two Angels Warn Lot	54
Isaac Is Born	56
Hagar and Ishmael Leave	58
God Tests Abraham	60
God Promises to Reward Abraham	64
Sarah Dies	65
Father of Many Nations	66
Abraham and Sarah's Descendants	67
About the Author	70

FOREWORD

Abram and his wife Sarai lived in the city of Ur in Mesopotamia. Sarai was very beautiful, but she was sad because she was unable to have children.

Abram had two brothers, Nahor and Haran, and a nephew named Lot. Abram's father served the gods of the land. But the one true God chose Abram to serve Him only.

God told Abram to leave his family and go to the land of Canaan, later known as Israel. And this is the story of Abram's journey of faith with God.

God Calls Abram

One day, while Abram was living in Mesopotamia, God spoke to him. He told him to leave his country and family, and go to the land He would show him. God promised to be very kind to Abram and to make him the father of a great nation.

"I will bless those who bless you and curse those who treat you with contempt. All the families on earth will be blessed through you." Genesis 12:3

Abram's Adventures Begin

Abram set off on the long journey to Canaan with his father, his wife, and his nephew Lot. They travelled along by the river Euphrates and lived in tents. When they reached Haran, they settled there for a while.

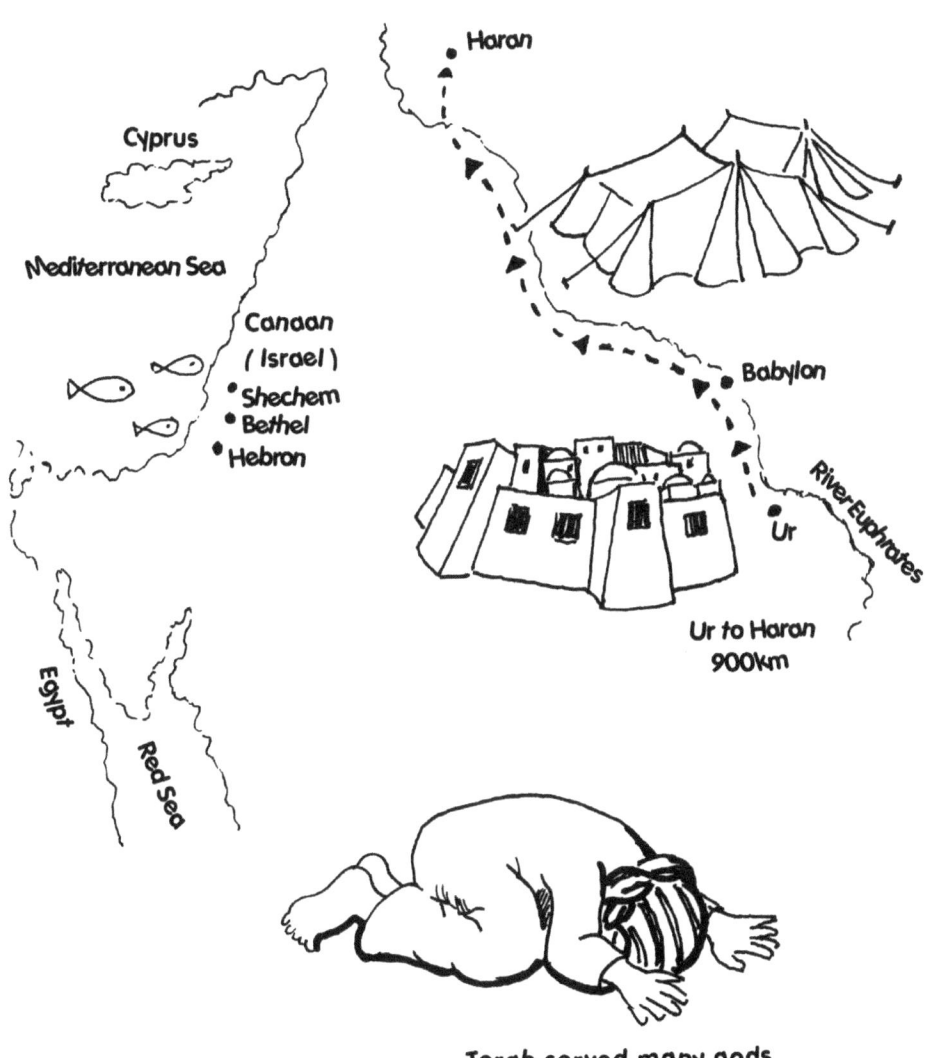

Abram's journey to Haran

Terah served many gods

Abram Arrives in Canaan

Abram stayed in Haran until his father died. Then he continued his journey to Canaan. Abram was seventy-five years old when he left Haran. And his nephew Lot chose to go with Abram and Sarai. When they arrived in Canaan, they travelled on to Shechem as far as the terebinth tree of Moreh.

Then the LORD appeared to Abram and said, "I will give this land to your descendants."   Genesis 12:7

Abram built an altar in the place where God had appeared to him.

Afterwards Abram travelled south and set up camp in the hill country, near Bethel. He built another altar to God there and worshipped Him.

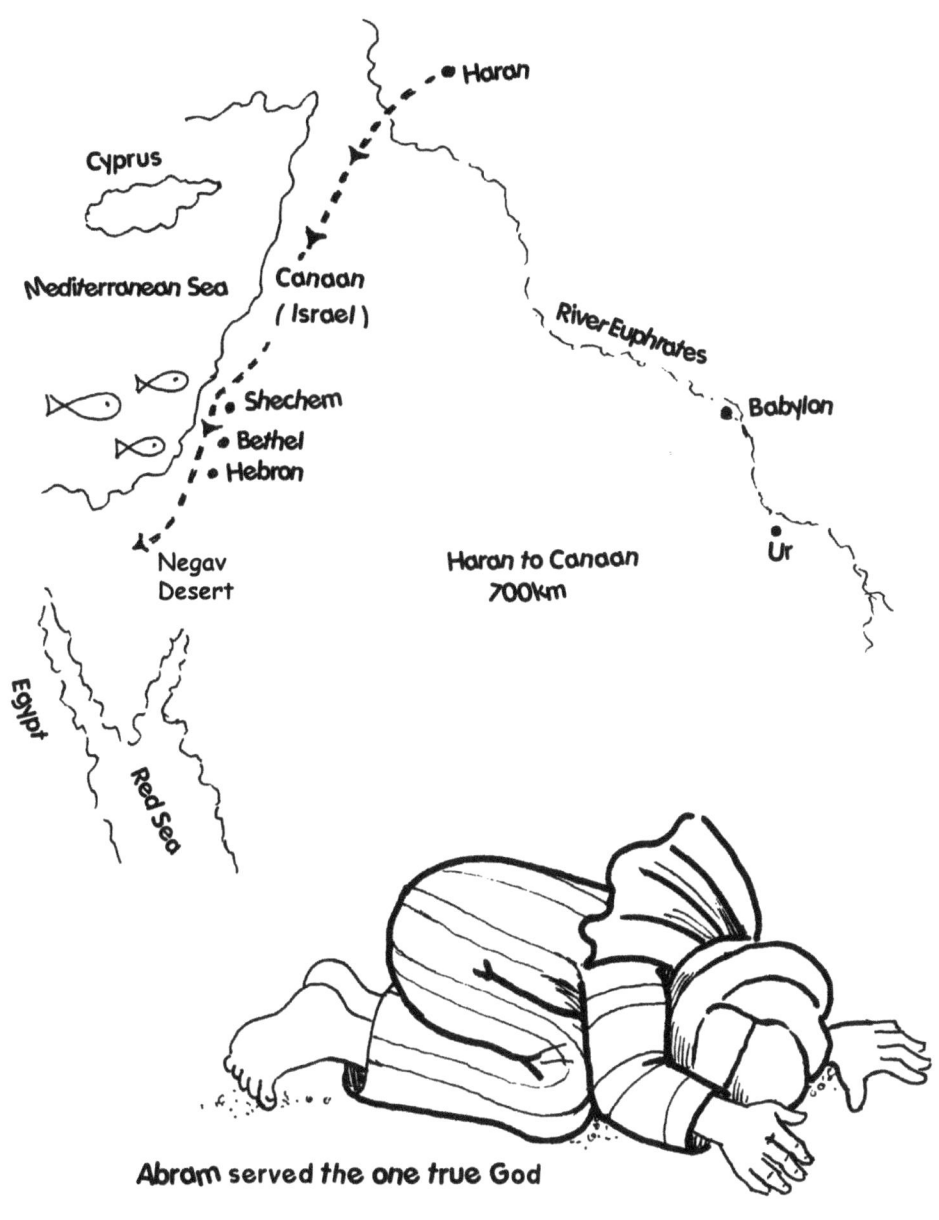

Abram served the one true God

Then he continued to travel south, towards the Negev.

Abram Goes Down to Egypt

At this time there was a famine in Canaan. So Abram decided to go down to Egypt where there was food. But he was afraid that the Egyptians would see his beautiful wife and kill him! So he pretended that she was his sister.

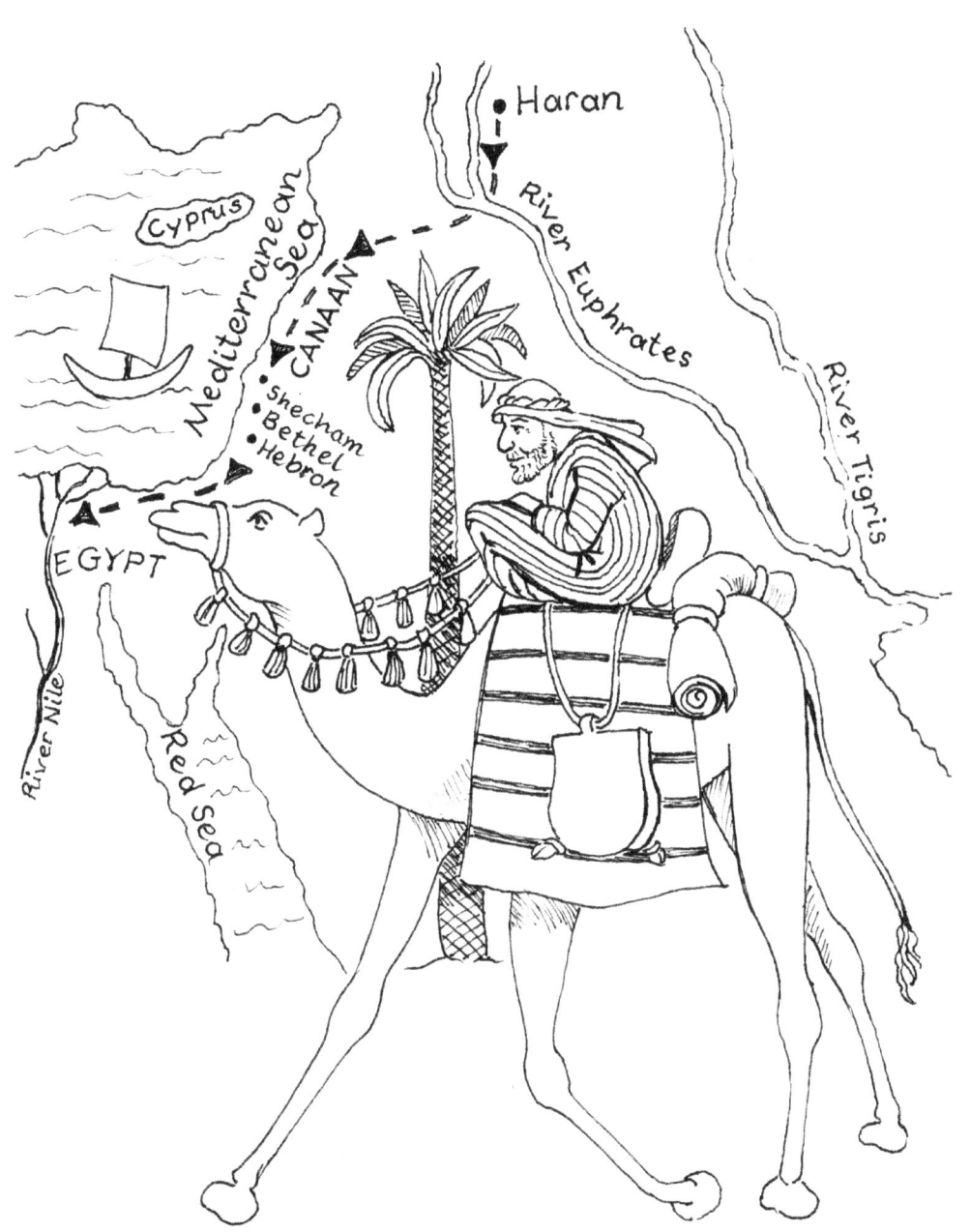

When Pharaoh heard about Sarai's beauty, she was taken to his palace. Then because of Sarai, the rich and powerful king was very generous towards Abram. He gave him herds of livestock, donkeys, male and female servants, and camels!

But Abram was very upset. His plot to save his life had gone badly wrong. He had lost his wife! If only he had trusted God to protect him instead of lying! He loved his wife and missed her. And without her, how could God's promise to give them a son come true?

God Frightens Pharaoh

Now God was very angry with Pharaoh for taking Abram's wife, and He frightened both him and his household with many terrible plagues. So in a panic, Pharaoh sent for Abram. But although he was angry, he did not harm Abram or Sarai. He told Abram to take his wife and to get out of Egypt!

Abram was delighted to have Sarai with him again. And he was a very rich man when they left Egypt. God had blessed him with silver and gold, and with everything that Pharaoh had given him.

Abram Returns to Canaan

Abram returned to the land that God had promised to his descendants and travelled north towards Bethel. When he arrived at the place where he had built an altar, he thanked God with all his heart. For it was God who had protected Abram and Sarai in Egypt, and also blessed them with great wealth.

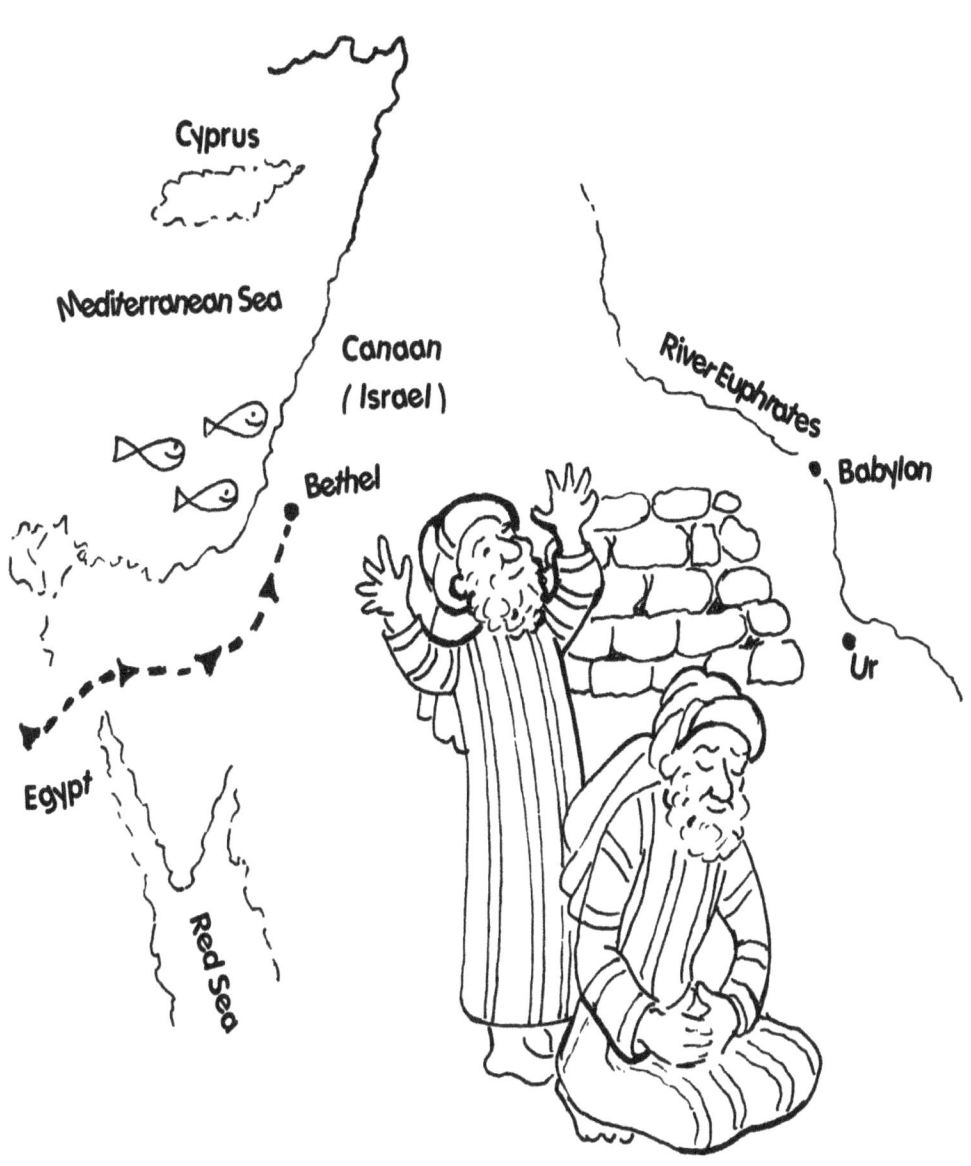

Abram and Lot Separate

Lot was still travelling with his uncle Abram, and both men had become very rich. But there wasn't enough pasture land to feed all their animals. So fights broke out between Abram and Lot's herdsmen.

Abram wanted to live in peace and suggested that he and Lot should separate. Abram asked his nephew to choose where he would like to live.

"The whole countryside is open to you. Take your choice of any section of the land you want, and we will separate. If you want the land to the left, then I'll take the land on the right. If you prefer the land on the right, then I'll go to the left."   Genesis 13:9

And Lot chose to go eastwards to the beautiful Jordan Valley, where there was plenty of water. Then he settled near Sodom and Gomorrah. But the men in those cities were very wicked and displeased the LORD.

Abram Stays in Canaan

Abram settled in Canaan and God was pleased with him. He promised to give Abram and his offspring the land of Canaan to keep forever. And God said that Abram's offspring would be like the dust of the earth, too numerous to count!

Then God told Abram to walk through the land He was giving to him.

So Abram moved on and camped at Hebron, where he built an altar to the LORD.

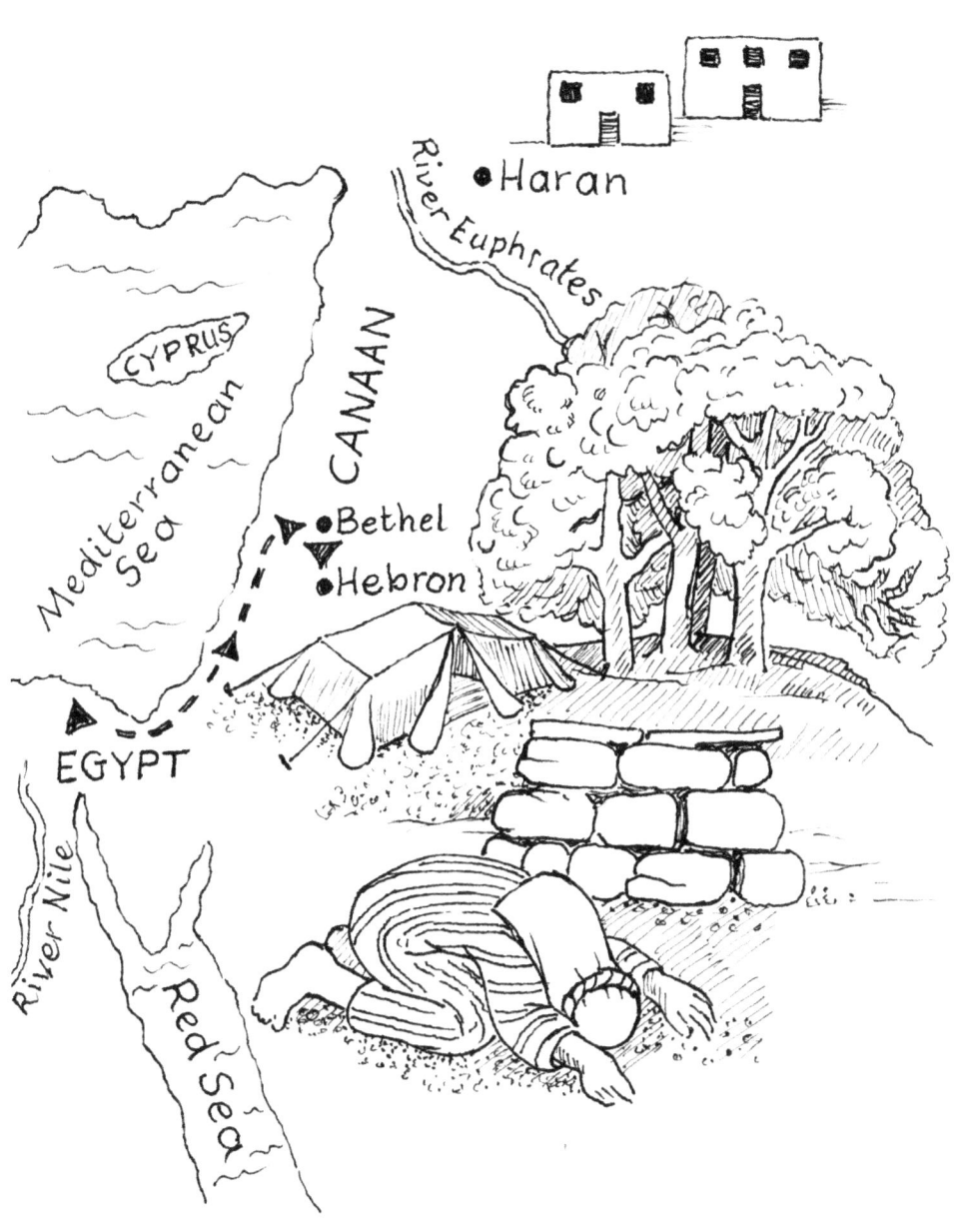

Abram never built a house in the land of Canaan. He lived in tents and kept on moving.

33

Lot Is Taken Captive

Around this time, four kings joined forces and attacked the five kings of the Jordan Valley. These four kings defeated the kings of Sodom and Gomorrah, plundered the two cities, and escaped to the mountains. Now Lot was no longer living in tents, but had settled in the city of Sodom. So he was taken captive, along with all his goods.

Abram Rescues Lot

When Abram the Hebrew heard that his nephew had been taken captive, he immediately took 318 male servants and chased after the invading armies, all the way to the town of Dan.

That night, Abram divided his men into two groups, then made a daring, surprise attack on the invaders' camp. When the enemy armies fled, Abram pursued them as far as Hobah, north of Damascus, successfully defeated them, and recovered all the captives and the stolen goods.

Abram Is Blessed by The King of Jerusalem

Melchizedek, the king of Salem and a priest of God Most High, brought Abram some bread and wine. Melchizedek blessed Abram with this blessing.

"Blessed be Abram by God Most High,
Creator of heaven and earth.
And blessed be God Most High,
who has defeated your enemies for you."
Genesis 14:18-20

Abram gave the king of Jerusalem a tenth of the plunder he had recovered.

On Abram's return, the king of Sodom came out to meet him in the King's Valley.

Then the king of Sodom asked Abram for his people, but said he could keep the plunder. However, Abram refused to take any reward. He didn't want anything at all from the wicked king of Sodom!

God Will Reward Abram

After this, God spoke to Abram. He said that He would protect Abram like a shield and give him a very great reward. But Abram was upset. What use were more gifts to him? He had no children and his servant would inherit everything he owned!

But God promised that Abram would have a son. He told him to look at the night sky, and said that his offspring would be as many as those shining stars! Abram believed God's promises and he was comforted.

Hagar and Ishmael

Sarai had not been able to have children. She had waited for God's promised son. But now she was an old woman and had lost all hope of having a family. So she gave her Egyptian maidservant to Abram. Then her maidservant, Hagar, had a son and named him Ishmael, meaning "God hears."

Sarai Will Have Her Own Son

God spoke again to Abram. He said that He would make him the father of many nations! His name would no longer be Abram. He would be called Abraham, which means "father of many."

And God said that his wife's name would no longer be Sarai. From then on she would be known as Sarah, meaning "princess." God promised that He would bless Sarah and give her a son. She would become the mother of many nations!

Now when Abraham heard this, he fell on his face and laughed to himself. He was now ninety-nine years old and Sarah was eighty-nine years old. Yet God was saying that this time next year their son would be born!

So Abraham asked God if Ishmael could be the son that He had promised.

But God replied, "No—Sarah, your wife, will give birth to a son for you. You will name him Isaac, and I will confirm my covenant with him and his descendants as an everlasting covenant."

(Genesis 17:19)

*Isaac - means, "he laughs."

And God said that He had already blessed Ishmael. He would have twelve princes and they would have many descendants.

However, His never-ending promise was with Isaac, the son that Sarah would have the following year.

That same day, God commanded Abraham to circumcise all the males in his household and all the slaves that he had bought, and Abraham did so.

Now Abraham was ninety-nine years old when he was circumcised and Ishmael was thirteen years old.

Abraham's Three Visitors

One day, Abraham was sitting in the doorway of his tent and he saw three men standing near the terebinth trees of Mamre. Abram ran to welcome these unexpected visitors. He bowed down before them and invited them to stay for a while. He said that water would be brought to them to wash their feet. And they could rest in the shade of the trees while a meal was being prepared for them.

As the men were eating, Abraham stood near them under the trees. When they asked him where Sarah was, Abraham replied that she was inside the tent.

Then one of them said, "I will return to you about this time next year, and your wife, Sarah, will have a son!" Genesis 18:10

Sarah was listening behind the tent curtains and she laughed to herself in dis-belief. She and her husband were too old to have a baby!

Then the LORD said to Abraham, "Why did Sarah laugh? Why did she say, 'Can an old woman like me have a baby?' Is anything too hard for the LORD? I will return about this time next year, and Sarah will have a son." Genesis 18:13-14

Then Sarah was afraid and said that she didn't laugh. But the LORD corrected her. He said that she did laugh.

Sodom and Gomorrah

When the three men got up to leave, Abraham walked a little way with them. Now the LORD said that He would not hide His plans from Abraham. So He told him that He was going to destroy the wicked cities of Sodom and Gomorrah.

Then Abraham was worried about Lot and his family. He begged the LORD to spare the cities for the sake of any good people living there. If there were fifty good people living in the city, would He spare it? And the LORD said He would. But there were not even ten good people living there! So the LORD went on His way. And Abraham went home.

Two Angels Warn Lot

It was evening when the two men arrived at Sodom, and Lot was sitting in the gateway of the city. Lot greeted the two strangers and invited them to spend the night at his home. But the angels said they were going to stay in the city's square. Now Lot knew that the city was a very dangerous place. So he insisted that they go with him. And the two angels accepted his invitation.

Lot made a meal for his guests. But before they went to bed, Lot's house was suddenly attacked by an unruly mob. And the angels struck these violent men with blindness, so they could not even find the door! Then the angels told Lot that the city was going to be destroyed. He and his family must flee, or they too would be killed! And Lot hurried to his future sons-in-law to warn them. But they just laughed!

At dawn the next morning, Lot was still lingering in the house. So the angels grabbed his hand, his wife's hand, and the hands of his two daughters, and led them out of the city. The angels warned them to keep running to the mountains and not to look back. But Lot begged them to let him go to a small village nearby, and so the angels agreed. Now as soon as the family arrived there, the LORD rained down fire and brimstone on Sodom and Gomorrah. But Lot's wife ignored the angels' warning and looked back. Then she was turned into a pillar of salt!

Isaac Is Born

As the LORD had promised, Sarah had a son. Abraham had waited a very long time for this miracle baby. He was one hundred years old when Isaac was born! But at last, Abraham and Sarah had a son. So their home was filled with joy and laughter.

The LORD kept His word and Sarah gave birth to a son.

Hagar and Ishmael Leave

Hagar looked down on her mistress, and Ishmael resented Isaac. So Sarah told Abraham to send them away. Now this upset Abraham, but God told him to do what Sarah had said. Abraham's descendants would come through Isaac. He should not worry about Ishmael, God would make him into a great nation.

So Abraham sent Hagar and Ishmael away with food and water. But travelling across the desert, the water ran out, and Ishmael fainted from thirst. Hagar left her son in the shade of a bush. Then she sat a little distance away from him because she didn't want to watch him die.

But God heard the boy crying, and the angel of God called to Hagar from heaven, "Hagar, what's wrong? Do not be afraid! God has heard the boy crying as he lies there. Go to him and comfort him, for I will make a great nation from his descendants."

Then God opened Hagar's eyes, and she saw a well full of water. She quickly filled her water container and gave the boy a drink. Genesis 21:17-19

Then they moved on and settled in the wilderness of Paran. God was with them and was kind to them. Ishmael became a skilled archer, and Hagar found an Egyptian wife for him, one of her own people. And from their descendants came the Arab nations.

God Tests Abraham

God knew how much Abraham loved Isaac. Yet He asked Abraham to offer up Isaac as a sacrifice to Him! Now this was a very difficult challenge for Abraham. Nevertheless, he was willing to obey God because he had learned that he could always trust Him. Besides, Isaac was going to inherit all the promises God had given to Abraham. So surely God wouldn't let him die!

God led Abraham to a high mountain. Then father and son climbed up the mountain together. Isaac carried the wood for the burnt offering, while Abraham carried coals in a clay pot and his knife. Isaac asked where the lamb was for the sacrifice, and Abraham said that God would provide a lamb.

When they reached the summit, Abraham built an altar and laid out the wood. Then he bound Isaac and laid him on the wood.

But it was not God's plan to hurt Isaac. He was testing Abraham's faith in Him. So when Abraham raised his knife, the Angel of the LORD called to him from Heaven.

"Don't lay a hand on the boy!" the angel said. "Do not hurt him in any way, for now I know that you truly fear God. You have not withheld from me even your son, your only son." Genesis 22:12

Then Abraham saw a ram caught by its horns in a thicket. So he took the ram and sacrificed it

God Promises to Reward Abraham

The Angel called to Abraham again.
He had not refused to give up his son,
so God would bless him with many descendants.
They would be like stars in the sky,
and sand on the seashore!
They would defeat their enemies.
And through them, all nations on earth would
be blessed, because he had obeyed God.

Sarah Dies

Now Abraham had lived as a stranger in the land that God had promised to give to him and his descendants. He owned no land there.

But when Sarah died, Abraham wanted a family burial place. So he bought the field of Machpelah and the cave that was in it. And Abraham buried Sarah in the cave.

Then Abraham sent his most trusted servant to his relatives in Mesopotamia, to find a wife for Isaac.

When Abraham's servant arrived at the city of Nahor, he stopped at the city's well. And God arranged that he should meet Rebekah there, the granddaughter of Abraham's brother.

Now God had chosen Rebekah to be Isaac's wife. And when Abraham's servant returned to Canaan, she went with him. Then Isaac took her as his bride. He loved Rebekah and was comforted after his mother's death.

Father of Many Nations

Then Abraham had six more sons with Keturah, his concubine. But Abraham gave all that he had to his son Isaac. He gave gifts to his other sons and sent them eastwards, away from Isaac.

God had blessed Abraham with a long life. He was one hundred and seventy-five years old when he died. And Isaac and Ishmael buried him with his wife Sarah, in the cave of Machpelah.

And just as God had promised, He had made Abraham the father of many nations. Through his son Isaac, Abraham was the father of the Jewish nation; and through his son Ishmael, he was the father of the Arab nations.

Abraham was also the father of the nations descended from Keturah's sons, Zimran, Jokshan, Medan, Midian, Ishbak, and Shuah.

So God kept His promise. He gave Abraham many descendants and all the nations of the earth have been blessed through him.

Abraham and Sarah's Descendants

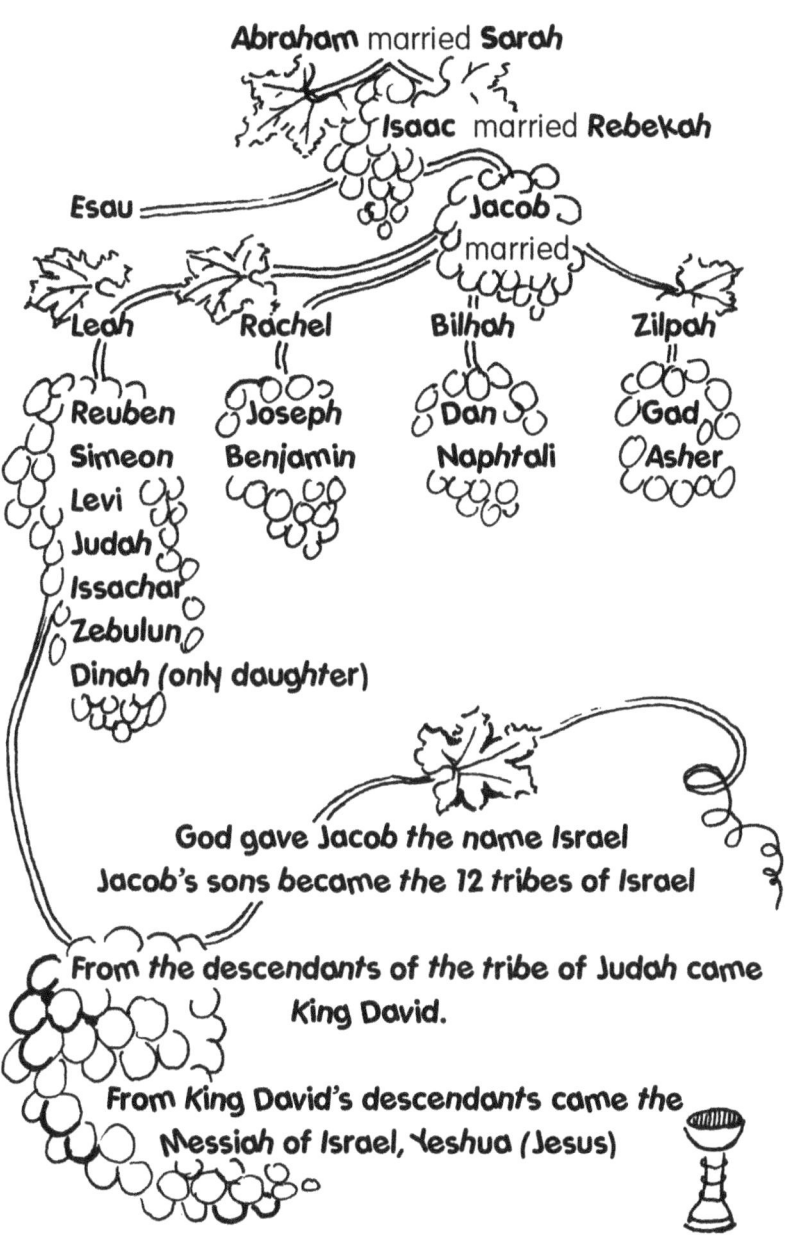

Abraham the Hebrew - Hebrew, Israelite, Jew, are names for the people of Israel.

The people of Israel were chosen to serve God.

"And now, Israel, what does the LORD your God require of you? He requires only that you fear the LORD your God, and live in a way that pleases Him, and love Him and serve Him with all your heart and soul." Deuteronomy 10:12

About the Author

God gave British author Pauline Shone a very special gift. It was the gift of creativity. And at seven years old, she made her first illustration, Prince Charming dancing with Cinderella! And at sixteen years of age, she began a five year Art College Degree Course. This led to a career in teaching, and then as a designer and sculptor for the ceramic industry. But after coming to a personal faith in Jesus as her Saviour, she used her God-given gift for Him. Over many years she created two series of illustrated Bible Stories for children.

Books by the Author

Feed My Lambs series, colouring books:

Feed My Sheep series for children ages 8-12
Illustrated Bible stories 8.5 x 11

illustrated Bible story books 6 x 9

Bible story in full colour hard cover

Bible study book for teens

Adult paperback books:

71

www.ingramcontent.com/pod-product-compliance
Lightning Source LLC
Chambersburg PA
CBHW040554010526
44110CB00054B/2706